SCHIZOPHRENIA

**A GUIDE FOR PEOPLE
WITH SCHIZOPHRENIA
AND THEIR FAMILIES**

**JANE PATERSON, MSW, CSW
DALE BUTTERILL, MSW, MPA
CLAUDIA TINDALL, MSW, CSW
DAVID CLODMAN, MSW, CSW
APRIL COLLINS, MSW, CSW**

This is a revised version of the
original guide written in 1988 by:
Ann Kerr, MSW, CSW
Ruth Thompson, MSW, CSW
Joel Jeffries, MB, FRCP(C)

Centre for Addiction and Mental Health
Centre de toxicomanie et de santé mentale

**A PAN AMERICAN HEALTH ORGANIZATION /
WORLD HEALTH ORGANIZATION COLLABORATING CENTRE**

Schizophrenia:
A Guide for People with Schizophrenia and Their Families

ISBN 0-88868-335-9

Product code: PM009

Printed in Canada
Copyright © 1999 Centre for Addiction and Mental Health

No part of this work may be reproduced or transmitted in any form or by any means electronic or mechanical, including photocopying and recording, or by any information storage and retrieval system without written permission from the publisher — except for a brief quotation (not to exceed 200 words) in a review or professional work.

For information on other Centre for Addiction and Mental Health resource materials or to place an order, please contact:

Marketing and Sales Services
Centre for Addiction and Mental Health
33 Russell Street
Toronto, Ontario M5S 2S1

Tel: 1 800 661-1111 or 416 595-6059 in Toronto
E-mail: marketing@camh.net

Web site: www.camh.net

Disponible en français sous le titre
La schizophrénie : Guide à l'intention des personnes atteintes de schizophrénie et de leur famille

2185 / 03-04   PM009

CONTENTS

Introduction 1

1 What is schizophrenia? 2

2 Treatment 8

3 Common concerns about schizophrenia and its treatment 12

4 The future 15

5 Discovering someone close to you has schizophrenia 19

6 Returning home: family concerns 26

Glossary 31

Appendices 34

ACKNOWLEDGMENT

We would like to thank those who were treated at the Clarke Institute of Psychiatry (one of the founding partners of the Centre for Addiction and Mental Health), and their families, for their questions, suggestions and comments on earlier versions of this guide. Also, our thanks are extended to the many Centre staff who were instrumental in producing this guide.

Dear Student:

Welcome to the fascinating work of assisting in the recovery of somebodies mental health.

Please read this booklet, cover-to-cover, so that I know you have a basic understanding of this illness.

Lucky you. I have also developed some test questions once you are finished. Just your luck.

I hope you enjoy this placement. Questions are permitted, even if you've read this booklet + forgotten a thing or two.

Regards,

Beth

INTRODUCTION

This guide is written for people with schizophrenia, their families and partners, and those who want a basic understanding of this illness. It is not a substitute for treatment from a physician, but it can be used as a basis for questions and discussion about schizophrenia.

- indicates that you may see this in the community or that I think it's important for you to know.

1 WHAT IS SCHIZOPHRENIA?

"I thought space aliens were after me. I didn't dare leave my room and covered all my windows with aluminum foil to keep them out. I refused to eat because I thought the food was poisoned."

The young woman quoted above has schizophrenia. She truly believed her delusion. No one could convince her otherwise. Not all people with schizophrenia will have the same type of experience as this woman's, but they will have some disturbances in thinking, feeling and relating to others.

At least one person in 100 can be expected to develop schizophrenia. Men and women are affected equally; however, men tend to experience their first episode in their late teens or early 20s. With women, the onset is usually a few years later.

How does schizophrenia begin and what is its course?

In most cases, schizophrenia can start so gradually that people experiencing symptoms, and their families, may not be aware of the illness for a long time. In some cases, however, the onset may be more rapid.

Phases of schizophrenia

There are three phases of schizophrenia — prodromal (or beginning), active, and residual. They tend to occur in sequence and appear in cycles throughout the course of the illness.

PRODROMAL PHASE

When symptoms develop gradually, people may begin to lose interest in their usual pursuits and to withdraw from friends and family members. They may become easily confused, have trouble concentrating, and feel listless and apathetic, preferring to spend most of their days alone. They may also become intensely preoccupied with religion or philosophy. Family and friends may be upset with this behaviour, believing the person is lazy rather than ill. Occasionally, these symptoms reach a plateau and do not develop further but, in most cases, an active phase of the illness follows. The prodromal period can last weeks or months.

Although the symptoms described above are typical of the prodromal phase of schizophrenia, they may also be due to other causes. If these symptoms are present, they should be discussed with a doctor.

ACTIVE PHASE

During schizophrenia's active phase, people may experience delusions, hallucinations, marked distortions in thinking and disturbances in behaviour and feelings. This phase most often appears after a prodromal period. On occasion, these symptoms can appear suddenly.

RESIDUAL PHASE

After an active phase, people may be listless, have trouble concentrating and be withdrawn. The symptoms in this phase are similar to those outlined under the prodromal phase. If there have been no symptoms before the first episode, few or no symptoms may be experienced afterward. During a lifetime, people with schizophrenia may become actively ill once or twice, or have many more episodes. Unfortunately, residual symptoms may increase, while ability to function normally may decrease, after each active phase. It is therefore important to try to avoid relapses by following the prescribed treatment. Currently it is difficult to predict at the onset how fully a person will recover.

WHAT ARE THE SYMPTOMS OF SCHIZOPHRENIA?

"When I first start becoming ill I lose my perspective on the things I hold important, such as courtesy toward my co-workers and roommate."

"When I'm ill lights are brighter, halls are longer and narrower, walls look like paper and colours are much more vivid. I see faces in the patterns of the rug which begin to have special meaning for me. If I'm lucky and my medication is increased, the symptoms may end here."

"Sometimes I feel like my arms and legs are disconnected from my body and that my body is disintegrating. I'm terrified to have a bath, because I'm afraid I will disintegrate and float down the drain. Sometimes I'm afraid that I'll fall apart if I take my clothes off."

— three first-hand accounts of various symptoms experienced by people with schizophrenia.

The symptoms of schizophrenia fall into two categories — "positive" and "negative" symptoms. The positive, or psychotic, symptoms most often associated with schizophrenia include delusions, hallucinations and grossly disorganized thought, mood and behaviour. Positive symptoms appear during active phases of the disorder. Negative symptoms — deficits in attention, memory, fluency of thought and language, emotional expression, judgment, decision-making and motivation — can be more persistent. These negative symptoms can lead to patterns of social withdrawal and alienation that may disrupt the person's ability to work and function normally.

People with schizophrenia will likely have one or more of the symptoms mentioned below. However, some of these symptoms are not unique to schizophrenia. It is always necessary to see a doctor for diagnosis.

Positive symptoms

At some phase of the illness, schizophrenia always involves delusions, hallucinations, disturbances in thinking, or disorganized behaviour.

DELUSIONS

Delusions are fixed, false beliefs that are not consistent with the person's culture, and have no basis in fact. Delusions may cause people to believe that their bodies or thoughts are being controlled by outside forces, that ordinary events have special meaning for them, that they are especially important or have unusual powers, or that their bodies have changed in some mysterious way. A common delusion experienced by people with schizophrenia is the belief that people are trying to harm them.

HALLUCINATIONS

Hallucinations are disturbances in perception. If people hear, see, taste, smell or feel something that does not actually exist, they are hallucinating. The most common hallucinations are auditory; that is, people will hear voices talking about them or to them. *Voices are often very mean, nasty, disturbing. Sometimes the voices are those of people they tried, other times they are not.*

Thought disorder is when a person's thoughts no longer connect in a way that makes it possible to communicate clearly with other people. Thoughts may be jumbled or they may seem to vanish temporarily. When talking, the person may jump from subject to subject and/or may have trouble communicating in a way that is clear and logical.

DISORGANIZED BEHAVIOUR

- A person with schizophrenia may have trouble completing everyday tasks such as bathing, dressing appropriately and preparing simple meals. During the acute phase of the illness, people will likely be unable to plan their days and follow through with tasks that they had previously performed effortlessly.

THE FOLLOWING SYMPTOMS MAY ALSO BE ASSOCIATED WITH SCHIZOPHRENIA:

- ### DISTURBANCES OF FEELING OR AFFECT (MOOD)

  At times people with schizophrenia may find it hard to express their feelings. On the one hand, they may experience inappropriate or intense bursts of feeling that seem to come out of the blue. On the other hand, they may feel empty of any emotions.

- ### AMBIVALENCE

  Ambivalence means having conflicting ideas, wishes and feelings toward a person, thing or situation. It may be hard for people with schizophrenia to make up their minds about anything, even relatively common decisions such as what to wear in the morning. Often, even if they are able to make a decision, it may be hard to stick with.

- ### SENSITIVITY

  One of the earliest symptoms in people with schizophrenia may be a change in their sensitivity toward others. They may become more sensitive and aware of other people, or they may withdraw and seem to pay no attention to others. They may become suspicious and worried that people are avoiding them, talking about them or feeling negatively toward them.

Negative symptoms

PHYSICAL SYMPTOMS

Physical activity may slow down in people with schizophrenia, sometimes to a point where they become motionless and stare into space. On rare occasions, they may become excited and overactive and experience strange body sensations.

REDUCED MOTIVATION

People with schizophrenia may have problems finishing tasks or making and carrying out long-term plans. They may also have less energy and drive, both before and after an active phase of illness.

SOCIAL WITHDRAWAL

People with schizophrenia may feel safer and calmer being alone. They may also become so absorbed in their own thoughts and sensations that they lose interest in the feelings and lives of others.

CHANGE IN HABITS AND ABILITY TO FUNCTION

People with schizophrenia may become less concerned about the way they dress and lose interest in grooming and bathing. They may find it increasingly difficult to carry out daily activities such as shopping or going to work.

What causes the illness?

Schizophrenia is now recognized as a disease of the brain. No single cause has been found. Current thinking is that schizophrenia results when genetic programming is impaired. This disrupts the chemistry of the developing brain of the fetus. Research into the chemical and genetic basis of schizophrenia has provided clues in the search for better ways to diagnose and treat the illness.

2 TREATMENT

Depending on how severe their symptoms are, people with schizophrenia may be treated as outpatients or they may be hospitalized. Today, the illness is treated primarily with a combination of medication and psychosocial interventions (counselling, for example). Family counselling is often recommended to help people with schizophrenia and their families understand and manage problems associated with the illness. It is important that they learn as much as possible about treatments being offered, understand the pros and cons of each treatment and discuss them with the physician so everyone becomes a partner in care.

Biological treatments

Medication

Medications called neuroleptics or antipsychotic drugs, developed in the 1950s, have proven to be among the most important medical advances for treating schizophrenia. Because of these drugs, people with schizophrenia no longer need to be hospitalized for years. Most are able to live in the community, needing hospitalization for the illness only if they relapse.

There are many different types of antipsychotic medications: the type and dosage will vary for each person. Most of these drugs are given in tablet form, some are liquids and others are given as injections. These medications are not addictive. It is important to keep taking the medication long enough to control symptoms and prevent a relapse. The treating physician will be able to determine how long the drug should be taken. Some people forget to take their medication regularly. For them, long-lasting (depot) injections may be given, sometimes just once a month.

Some people do not respond to traditional antipsychotic medications, but may get good results from recently developed medications. One of the newer drugs, clozapine, can weaken immunity in some people. Therefore, people taking clozapine need regular blood tests to monitor their white cell counts.

Antipsychotic medications are the main class of drugs used to treat schizophrenia, but other types of medication may also be prescribed to treat particular symptoms such as depression, anxiety or sleep difficulties.

SIDE-EFFECTS

Unpleasant side-effects may be experienced when taking antipsychotic medication. This is especially common during the active phase of illness, when a higher dose of medication may be required. The most common problems include muscular stiffness, tremor, muscle spasms, restlessness, dry mouth and blurred vision. As a result of these side-effects, people may become discouraged, and may not want to take medication. However, over time the body tends to adjust and the side-effects should lessen. Other medication may also be prescribed to relieve or reduce these unpleasant side-effects.

For some, long-term use of neuroleptic medication results in another disorder called tardive dyskinesia. It usually consists of involuntary movements of the face, eyes, tongue, mouth or jaw. If this condition appears, medication may be changed or discontinued.

Electroconvulsive therapy (ECT)

Electroconvulsive therapy (ECT), often referred to as electro-shock therapy or shock treatment, is not usually recommended for the treatment of schizophrenia. However, in some cases it is prescribed for people who are severely ill and do not respond to medication. It may also be prescribed for people who are severely depressed.

Psychosocial interventions

Schizophrenia usually develops in young people during the years when they would normally develop the skills needed for independent living. Because this process is disrupted by the onset of their illness, psychosocial interventions are often used to help develop these crucial skills. Psychosocial interventions help people set and achieve goals in key areas of their lives. A variety of approaches are used, such as case management, counselling, centre or clubhouse-based programs, and housing programs with built-in support or flexible outside support.

Case management

Case managers are clinicians who are trained in psychosocial rehabilitation. They link people to agencies and services, communicate with families and other caregivers, and monitor the individual's satisfaction and progress. They address a wide range of needs to help their clients achieve the best possible quality of life within the community. Their work may include help with housing, vocational, social, educational and financial needs, or crisis intervention — depending on their clients' needs at any given time. In addition to co-ordinating these services, case managers may also act as counsellors and therapists. They may also be a link with medical services, to address such issues as medication and other medical needs. Case management services are flexible; each program is tailored to and wholly directed by the clients and their needs.

COUNSELLING

Counselling is offered by health care professionals trained in social work, nursing, psychology, medicine, or occupational therapy. The most common form of counselling for people with schizophrenia is supportive psychotherapy, which can be provided individually or in group formats. Using this approach, people learn more about the sources of their distress and receive help to change beliefs and behaviours that contribute to their problem. Emphasis is placed on encouraging people to develop their strengths and their ability to cope with illness.

- Proper nutrition — if one is to heal, + stay healthy.
  - including vitamins
  - may need food sensitivity testing, hair analysis to determine what other stressors are at play — Add ing to stress load — overall.
- Sleep — are they getting enough?
  - if not explore why not. Less too much water drinking @ night; caffeine drinks too late in the day, no way to relax, poor sleep hygiene.)
- Exercise — is this in balance? Explore what might work, what they enjoyed in the past, walking/cycling groups, mall walkies, get off bus one stop early + walk, park further away + walk, team sports, part of daily routine.
  wkly

3 COMMON CONCERNS ABOUT SCHIZOPHRENIA AND ITS TREATMENT

Will I need to be hospitalized?

If, during an active phase of schizophrenia, you are frightened, disorganized, violent or suicidal, admission to hospital will probably be recommended for your own care and protection. If the symptoms of illness are not too severe, treatment on an outpatient basis may be possible, especially if the health care professionals providing treatment are familiar with you and your illness.

Can I be kept in the hospital against my will?

In Ontario, you cannot be admitted and kept in hospital against your will unless you are in danger of harming yourself or others, or are unable to care for yourself. In such a case, you may be found mentally incapable of giving consent to being treated, and may then be committed to hospital involuntarily. If this happens, you will be visited by a Rights Advisor, who will explain your legal rights. This service is free. If you are a patient in one of Ontario's provincial psychiatric hospitals, you may obtain free advice and representation from a psychiatric patient advocate located in the hospital.

The laws applying in any given area can be discussed with your therapist. People who live outside of Ontario can contact their local mental health association for further information.

Is outpatient treatment necessary?

You will probably be discharged from hospital after the active phase is over, when you are well enough to manage in the community. You will need to see your physician as long as medication is required. Treating physicians may be psychiatrists or general practitioners. Besides doctors, you may see other mental health professionals. These may include social workers, nurses, psychologists or occupational therapists, who will help plan and carry out treatment programs. Even if symptoms disappear, it is important to have professionals you can call if you have concerns about your condition.

WILL I SUFFER A RELAPSE ?

Although some people have only one episode of schizophrenia, schizophrenia can be a condition that includes relapses. It is important to be aware of stresses that trigger relapses so these can be reduced or avoided. It is important to seek treatment as soon as symptoms return. If you stop your medication too soon, your chances of relapsing increase significantly.

ARE ALL UNCOMFORTABLE FEELINGS DUE TO SCHIZOPHRENIA?

No, not all uncomfortable feelings are symptoms of illness. After active phases of schizophrenia, you may feel sad, angry, ashamed, guilt-ridden, inadequate or anxious about the future. These feelings are quite natural and it is helpful to discuss them with a therapist, family member or friend. Sometimes, people who have schizophrenia may be so afraid of relapse that they withdraw and become fearful of trying new things. This is understandable but it is important to find the support, courage and confidence necessary to achieve the best possible quality of life.

What should be done if I feel suicidal or have thoughts of harming others?

Tell your doctor immediately if you feel suicidal or have thoughts of physically harming others. If you do not have a doctor, or if the doctor is not available, go or get someone to take you to the emergency department of the nearest general or psychiatric hospital for help.

Will alcohol, coffee or other drugs affect my schizophrenia?

A large number of people with schizophrenia use alcohol and non-prescription drugs, either alone or in combination. They find that the short-term effects of these substances help to "numb" their symptoms or to "kill time." However, substance use can interfere with how your medication works, and can have a range of negative consequences. Street drugs can worsen the symptoms of schizophrenia, even in people who are already taking antipsychotic medication. Substance use should be avoided at all costs.

Alcohol, taken in conjunction with antipsychotic medication, has a sedating effect that causes drowsiness. It is extremely risky to drive or work around heavy machinery if antipsychotic medications are combined with alcohol.

Caffeine and similar stimulants are found in tea, coffee, cola drinks and, to some degree, in chocolate. If you are taking antipsychotic medication, you may find that caffeine intensifies the side-effects of your medication, particularly restlessness. If a large quantity of caffeine is consumed, it may also interfere with how effective your medication is.

4 THE FUTURE

TREATMENT CHOICES

As with any illness, it is important that you understand the specific ways that your illness affects you. There are many treatment choices to make and it is important to be as well informed as possible regarding treatment options. You can collaborate with health care providers and others to choose the programs that will be best for your recovery.

There are also many consumer/survivor organizations throughout the country. These organizations can be very helpful in providing support, information and friendship.

COURSE AND OUTCOME

- Schizophrenia takes a tremendous toll, both on the people with the illness and on their families. However, today there is reason to be optimistic. Major technical advances have contributed greatly to how we understand the biology of schizophrenia and its treatment.

It is true that many people suffer from intense and long-lasting symptoms of schizophrenia, but the disease does not always progress to a deteriorated state. Although no present treatment approach can prevent or cure schizophrenia, some have had remarkable effects on the course of the illness. With the arrival of new medication options, many people have experienced greater symptom control, so that rehabilitation is possible.

- **WORK AND STUDY**

Some people recover fully, return to their jobs or finish school; others find they cannot cope with their jobs or studies after an active phase of schizophrenia. If you want to work but wonder if you can cope, find out about programs in vocational rehabilitation. Such programs are a chance to rebuild work skills and self-confidence, and to identify occupations that suit your changed circumstances. Full-time, paid work is not the only option. Many people with schizophrenia are able to improve the quality of their lives even if they are not employed.

HAVING CHILDREN

The possibility of someone in the general population having schizophrenia is about one in 100. If one parent has schizophrenia the chance is about one in 10; if both parents have schizophrenia the chances are four in 10. Raising children can be stressful for anyone. This is often particularly true for people with schizophrenia. These factors need to be seriously considered before planning a pregnancy. If you are thinking about having children, you should discuss the matter thoroughly with your partner and your doctor.

FAMILY INVOLVEMENT IN TREATMENT

Families can help people with schizophrenia recover and stay well. It is usually a good idea for partners and family members to meet doctors and/or other health care providers to learn about and discuss the illness. They may be asked to discuss what the person with schizophrenia was like before the prodromal phase of illness, to ensure accurate diagnosis and appropriate treatment.

Families are often troubled by changes in the behaviour of people with schizophrenia during the active phase of illness. Most families want to help, especially if their concerns are understood and discussed with the person with schizophrenia and his or her treatment team. If people with schizophrenia need help to care for themselves and organize their lives, their partners or relatives may need to step in to guide and protect them. The struggle to find the right balance between being dependent and being independent may be upsetting both to people with schizophrenia and to their families. This balance is apt to change at the different phases of illness. People with schizophrenia need to be patient with themselves and with their families, and work at ways to get along. Sometimes a family therapist can help.

Staying well

People with schizophrenia and their families should discuss ways to keep symptoms under control and to live a full life. It is also important to take the following steps:

- Learn about schizophrenia and its treatment; ask the doctors or therapists about any aspects you do not understand.
- Arrange medical follow-up and stay on prescribed medication long enough to prevent a relapse.
- Get help to cope with everyday situations by talking with a therapist or by going to a rehabilitation program.
- Contact your doctor or therapist immediately if symptoms return or get worse.
- Learn to cope with stress by gradually increasing the amount you can handle until you are living close to your potential. Determine how much stress is too much and when it is necessary to draw back. Finding the correct balance is difficult, but it can be learned.

- Have at least one person to rely on and confide in. It may help if you stay in touch with family members and/or join self-help groups, religious organizations or consumer groups.
- Develop a well-balanced lifestyle that includes regular exercise, rest, healthy meals, as well as time for friends, family and fun. If you are married and you have schizophrenia, you should assume as much responsibility for your family as you can. If you are able, you should work or become involved in activities such as social rehabilitation programs.

5 DISCOVERING SOMEONE CLOSE TO YOU HAS SCHIZOPHRENIA

"I couldn't believe our sensible, studious daughter. She had changed into a person I hardly recognized. She refused to change her clothes and said she heard voices telling her she was evil and deserved to die."

Many family members say that the greatest challenge in their lives has been learning to cope after someone close to them develops schizophrenia. For the first few months, especially in the active phase, people with schizophrenia, their families, and people in their social network may be troubled by their worry, disappointment and grief. The danger of families and relationships splitting apart under the stress of facing a serious illness can be all too real.

It is important for family members, partners and friends to talk to each other openly about their concerns and to find ways to support each other during this difficult time. Professional counselling can help alleviate tension and distress.

In spite of the many difficulties, most family members usually manage to rally together, to learn about the illness, to come to terms with their concerns for the future and their sense of loss, and to work toward the rehabilitation of the person with schizophrenia.

Some people recover from their first active phase of schizophrenia and stay well; others are not so fortunate. Whatever happens, people with the illness and their families need to find ways to live their lives as fully as possible.

Family concerns about schizophrenia

As a family member or friend of a person with schizophrenia, you may find the illness distressing, especially during the active phase. The first episode can be particularly upsetting if you do not know what is wrong or how to help. Most hospitals have trained staff who will talk about what is happening and who can offer some guidance.

Schizophrenia is not caused by family pressure or parental errors. When people with schizophrenia are ill, they may become so absorbed in their strange, sometimes frightening, inner world that they lose interest in their work or studies. In some cases, they may turn away from partners or family members or become hostile. In other cases, they may cling to family members and not want to let them out of their sight.

You may feel intense pity, compassion, love, fear, anger, resentment, guilt, even hatred toward the person with schizophrenia. Such feelings are common and understandable. It is useful to talk about these feelings with people you trust. You need the comfort and support of other family members and friends during this time.

Finding treatment

If people are experiencing some of the symptoms described earlier in this guide, they should seek psychiatric help as soon as possible. They may not understand the need for treatment, but as a family member, partner or friend you should urge them to go to a doctor, community psychiatrist, or the emergency department of the nearest psychiatric or general hospital. Depending on the severity of symptoms, treatment may be recommended on an outpatient basis or in hospital.

Most people with schizophrenia want treatment and can be persuaded to accept it. Others, whose judgment is seriously impaired, may not recognize that they are ill. This makes it difficult for them, if they refuse to accept the help they need, and for their family members, who recognize the need for treatment.

If people with schizophrenia refuse psychiatric help, family doctors, the local psychiatric hospitals or public health departments can give you information and advice about how to handle the situation. If there is a risk of self-harm or harm to others, you can phone the police or go to a Justice of the Peace. In most communities, the police are authorized to take ill people to hospital for an examination if they observe dangerous behaviour, or if they have either a doctor's certificate or a judicial warrant from a Justice of the Peace. *A contentious issue tho.*

WHAT TO DO WHEN A RELATIVE IS IN HOSPITAL

"I was initially kept in the dark and didn't know what they were doing to my son in the hospital. I was terribly worried and felt much better after the initial interviews were over. The sooner the interviews take place, the better."

— a mother

"His doctor wouldn't speak to us and we didn't find out why until later. The reason for confidentiality should be explained by hospital staff."

— a wife and a son

We educate families on how to talk to the individual's doctor, e, the [busy?] nature of that relationship, if no consent is given.

During the first hospitalization, you may learn for the first time that your relative has schizophrenia. It is important to realize that schizophrenia is an illness that can be treated. You may be extremely upset about the diagnosis, and need to talk about your feelings and concerns. Most hospitals have social workers or other professionals on staff who are available to talk with families.

Visits are usually encouraged, but to begin with, hospital staff often recommend that they be brief. To avoid frustration, you and other family members may want to take turns visiting. Each hospital ward has its own visiting hours. You can help by learning ward routines. You can also help by reassuring the ill person that hospitalization is needed for proper assessment and treatment.

Family members are often asked for information, because people with schizophrenia are often too frightened or disturbed to give an accurate picture of the development of their illness. Some people may refuse to allow hospital staff to contact their families. If this happens, hospital staff, like family doctors, have no alternative but to abide by their clients' wishes. However, families are able to contact hospital staff and voice their concerns.

FAMILY INVOLVEMENT

In recent years, hospital staff have become increasingly aware that families are important partners in treatment. People with schizophrenia, their families and mental health professionals need to work together toward recovery. It is also important that family members feel they are listened to and understood because they have major and sometimes difficult adjustments to make as a result of the illness.

You will probably have questions and concerns about various aspects of the illness and its treatment. It is important for you and the ill person to know what is happening. You should not hesitate to ask for information from hospital staff. It also helps people with schizophrenia when they hear their illness openly discussed. The ill relative will probably be included in family counselling sessions as soon as the active phase is over.

Medication and side-effects

When the ill person starts taking medication, you may be distressed to see side-effects such as drowsiness or restlessness. What seems most difficult for many families to deal with is the stiff, "zombie-like" look that people taking medication sometimes develop. Medication changes can be made. The initial dose can be lowered or another drug can be prescribed to take away the stiffness. In spite of the side-effects, it is important that medication be taken so that symptoms clear.

Leaving hospital too soon

Sometimes ill people want to leave hospital before their treatment is completed. This can have serious repercussions, because the illness can worsen and they will need to return to hospital. You should strongly urge them to stay in hospital until hospital staff agree it is time for discharge. However, if ill people are not suicidal, nor threatening others, or if they are able to care for themselves, they cannot be forced to remain in hospital, even if their decision is contrary to medical advice.

Relating to an acutely ill person

You may not know what to say to the acutely ill person. In the active phase of schizophrenia, people may feel their minds are being bombarded from all directions by ideas, questions and commands. They may feel too overwhelmed to sort out even minor problems. Generally speaking, you should try to be as supportive and understanding as possible, and to speak in a calm, clear and straightforward manner. When necessary, you can help to reduce stress by relieving the ill person's responsibilities.

People with schizophrenia may use words that sound like nonsense to others. If they cannot be understood, you should try to communicate your interest and concern in other ways. You can listen to music, paint, watch television or sit quietly together. You will soon learn what works best by noticing the person's responses to what you do together. Never talk as if the ill person is not there. People with schizophrenia are usually aware of what is going on around them, even if they appear not to be listening.

Living arrangements

As a person with schizophrenia improves, hospital staff, especially social workers, may talk to family members about living arrangements. Some people return home, some go to group homes and still others find rooms and apartments of their own. Each family must make its own decision. It is not unusual to try one living plan and then another. It is often helpful to discuss what kind of accommodation is available and what could be most helpful to the ill person at different stages of recovery.

Where people do best

People with schizophrenia seem to do best in well-organized home environments with regular routines that include meals, sleep, work and recreation. They also do best when living with people (either family members, friends or group-home employees) who are calm, matter-of-fact and warm without getting too close. Sometimes they can tolerate only limited emotional involvement with family members, even those with whom they have previously been close.

Some concerned families are naturally low-key in the way they express themselves; others are excitable and over-anxious. Family members and friends need to learn how to visit or live with a person with schizophrenia. Even if your family is naturally calm and supportive, you will need information and guidance when dealing with the illness for the first time.

6 RETURNING HOME: FAMILY CONCERNS

WHAT FAMILIES SAY THEY NEED AND WANT

Upon return from hospital, people with schizophrenia and their families face many challenges. Below is a list of things various families have said were most helpful when their ill relatives returned to the community:

- journals and books about schizophrenia
- talking to the ill relative to learn about the illness
- support from people in their social network
- case management support
- a support group, such as the Schizophrenia Society
- a job for the ill person to go to
- contact with hospital staff and family doctor
- a good sense of humour
- police support.
- the part about a wonderful, resourceful, spot on O.T., must have been omitted in error. Reinsert here.

STRESSORS AFTER DISCHARGE

When people are discharged from hospital after the active phase of schizophrenia, some symptoms may remain. They may be withdrawn and prefer to spend time alone. They may be preoccupied with their own thoughts and fantasies, leading to problems with concentration. Personal grooming may slip. They may sleep during the day and be up at night. Interest and energy for activities they previously enjoyed may disappear. They may resent being reminded of daily routines.

You may find these behaviours and attitudes very stressful. As a result, it is important to find ways for your ill relative to carry out his or her responsibilities. It is helpful to set reasonable expectations and to <u>work out a structured approach to accomplishing tasks.</u> *Ask your doctor about obtaining the services of an occupational therapist.*

Social contacts

It is common for people with schizophrenia to feel uncomfortable in the presence of others, especially as they recover from the effects of an active phase. Interpersonal contact can be very difficult for a number of reasons, including fear of people, lack of confidence, and feelings of inadequacy or being different from others. You need to understand these problems, but at the same time you need to emphasize the importance of social contact to the person's health. Encouraging them to "do their best" and helping to set up structured interactions can benefit people with schizophrenia. Just carrying on with regular family activities helps build up tolerance for interaction with others.

Finding the right pace

It will take time for you and your ill relative to establish a pace that supports recovery. Often you may be "out of sync" with each other, with one or the other moving too quickly or too slowly. To get "in sync" it may be helpful for everyone to negotiate a daily routine that includes elements of self-responsibility, activity and social contact.

You can help by being open and supportive to the ill relative's efforts to reconstruct his or her life. Recognizing that people do things differently will prevent needless arguments over the "right way" to perform a task.

- Suggestions regarding inappropriate behaviour will be heard more easily if they are delivered in a low-key manner. It helps to emphasize the positive. You may need to provide more input and perform more tasks in the early stages of recovery. As the ill person progresses, you will need to do less.

FAMILY RELATIONSHIPS

Coping with schizophrenia may raise a variety of issues and needs for different family members, depending on their relationship to the person with schizophrenia. For example, children of a parent with schizophrenia are likely to be confused and upset by their parent's changed behaviour. They may be afraid, hurt or ashamed. When schizophrenia affects children, parents will often feel guilty and burdened.

The needs of siblings are sometimes overlooked. Like parents, siblings may feel self-blame and guilt. It is also common for siblings to be afraid of becoming ill themselves. Supportive family counselling can help all family members to address their needs and concerns.

COUPLES

Support is critical to the well-being of ill people. It is important that couples in which one partner has schizophrenia find ways of maintaining and expressing their affection for each other. Task sharing is an important element of primary relationships. If couples can agree on what tasks ill partners perform as they recover, it will be easier to move forward. If the ill person cannot act as a confidante, his or her partner should seek an alternative source of support, possibly through a relative's group. If a couple experience ongoing difficulty in their relationship, couple counselling should be considered.

THE NEEDS OF THE FAMILY

You need the support of relatives and friends to cope effectively. Keep in mind that all family members are important and have their own needs. You need to find a balance — which will vary according to the changing circumstances of your lives. If you don't take time for yourself, you risk becoming exhausted or "burned out." Other people, such as friends, therapists and the clergy, may be willing to help and should be called upon when the need arises.

DISAGREEMENTS

At times you and your ill relative will disagree. The best way to handle disagreements is to make sure that the ill person's point of view is made clear. This will avoid any misunderstanding in perspectives. By stating thoughts and feelings calmly and matter-of-factly, it is more likely that you will resolve your differences of opinion constructively. It will not help to give in to unreasonable demands out of sympathy or fear.

AGGRESSIVE BEHAVIOUR

Most people with schizophrenia would never harm anyone. In fact, they tend to be timid. However, a person with schizophrenia may make threats or strike out in response to hallucinations and delusions. This can be surprising and frightening to those around him or her. Aggressive behaviour toward others often results when people with schizophrenia think others are hostile, or when they feel crowded or trapped.

If they are upset, do not trivialize their feelings. Do not tease, insult or nag them. Do not to get too close either emotionally or physically. If violent threats are made, remain calm and take steps to ensure your safety. Help from friends, neighbours or the police may be necessary. Therapists should be informed, and can give you ideas to prevent or deal with similar episodes in the future.

You and the person with schizophrenia can learn to deal with anger and conflict in a constructive manner. You may meet with therapists to talk about how to prevent violent episodes in the future. Some hospitals and outpatient clinics offer family education programs to help relatives learn coping and communication strategies.

DEPRESSION AND SUICIDE ATTEMPTS

- Some people with schizophrenia feel depressed, unlovable and hopeless. Occasionally, they may be in serious danger of taking their own lives. This is most common in young men during the first five years of their illness. Suicidal thoughts may also be a sign of relapse. People considering suicide often talk about it.

- If your relative expresses such thoughts or ideas, they should be taken seriously and discussed with the person's therapist.* If the therapist cannot be reached, take the person to the emergency department of the hospital where treatment was previously provided, or to the nearest general or psychiatric hospital. The risk of suicide may make family members overly cautious. Conversely, some families underestimate the risk. Encourage the ill person to share any feelings of depression as possible warning signs. If you can recognize suicidal thinking, you will be more prepared to act quickly and competently in times of crisis.

ORGANIZATIONS FOR FAMILIES AND FRIENDS

Many families and friends join support or self-help organizations where they can meet others who are struggling with the same problems. Members learn from and support each other at all stages of care. See Appendix 2 for names and addresses of support groups.

GLOSSARY

This section provides definitions for some of the medical terms used in this guide, as well as other words that you may encounter in connection with schizophrenia.

ACTIVE PHASE OF SCHIZOPHRENIA – short, intense episodes of the illness in which most of its severe symptoms are manifest.

AGRANULOCYTOSIS – failure of the bone marrow to produce neutrophil white blood cells that fight infection; agranulocytosis is a possible adverse effect of clozapine.

AMBIVALENCE – simultaneously experiencing opposing or conflicting emotions, attitudes, ideas or wishes toward a person or situation.

ANHEDONIA – an inability to experience pleasure.

ANTIPSYCHOTIC MEDICATION – medications used in the treatment of schizophrenia. Formerly known as major tranquilizers.

ANXIOLYTICS – medications used to reduce severe anxiety, tension and agitation. Previously known as minor tranquilizers.

AUTISM – a state of mind characterized by daydreaming, fantasies and disregard for external reality.

BLOCKING – when a person's train of thought suddenly stops, even in the middle of a sentence.

FLAT OR BLUNT AFFECT – exhibiting little emotion and having an expressionless face.

INCONGRUOUS AFFECT – an inappropriate display of emotions, for instance, laughing when talking about sad events.

NEGATIVISM – an attitude characterized by ignoring, resisting or opposing suggestions from other people.

NEUROLEPTICS – medications used in the treatment of schizophrenia that have antipsychotic effects. Formerly known as major tranquilizers.

PARKINSONISM – a side-effect of neuroleptics characterized by awkward and stiff facial and arm movements.

PRODROMAL PHASE OF SCHIZOPHRENIA – the period of time leading up to an active phase of schizophrenia. It can vary in length depending on the individual.

REALITY TESTING – ability to distinguish reality from unreality. Poor reality testing is the inability to determine where fantasy ends and reality begins.

RESIDUAL PHASE OF SCHIZOPHRENIA – the long period of time following the active phase of illness in which symptoms are much less severe or almost disappear.

SCHIZO-AFFECTIVE DISORDER – concurrent symptoms of both schizophrenia and affective disorder. Affective disorders are characterized by disturbances of mood such as depression and elation. The two main categories are depressive and manic-depressive illness/bipolar affective disorder.

SCHIZOID – abnormally shy, aloof, sensitive and withdrawn, to the point that normal functioning is impaired.

TARDIVE DYSKINESIA – a possible side-effect of antipsychotic medication, usually after prolonged use. It usually consists of involuntary movements of the tongue, face, eyes, mouth or jaw, of which the person may not be aware. If tardive dyskinesia appears, the neuroleptic may need to be changed or discontinued.

THOUGHT DISORDER – when the continuity of thought is broken so that the person is not able to carry through a line of thinking in a way that makes sense to other people.

APPENDIX 1

Over the years, different types of schizophrenia have been described in a number of ways. The following classifications have been taken from the *Diagnostic and Statistical Manual of Mental Disorders* (fourth edition) – DSM-IV.

1. **DISORGANIZED TYPE** – Obvious personality disorganization marked by incoherence and a flat, silly affect. Other common features are making faces, odd mannerisms, preoccupation with bodily complaints and wanting to be left alone.

2. **CATATONIC TYPE** – Marked disturbance in physical activity, either a long period of immobility in a strange position or uncontrollable excitement.

3. **PARANOID TYPE** – Belief that others are plotting against them and persecuting them. May exhibit unreasonable jealousy or think they are unusually powerful and important. Auditory hallucinations (hearing voices) may accompany these ideas.

4. **UNDIFFERENTIATED TYPE** – Psychotic symptoms that cannot be found in the above categories. Symptoms from more than one category.

5. **RESIDUAL TYPE** – Symptoms of schizophrenia which remain after an active episode.

APPENDIX 2

ORGANIZATIONS FOR FAMILIES AND CONSUMERS

Schizophrenia Society of Canada
Canadian National Office
75 The Donway West
Don Mills, Ontario M3C 2E9   Phone (416) 445-8204

Ontario Friends of Schizophrenics
885 Don Mills Road, Suite 322
North York, Ontario M3C 3Z2   Phone (416) 449-6830

The National Alliance for the Mentally Ill
2101 Wilson Boulevard, Suite 302
Arlington, Virginia   Phone (703) 524-7600
U.S.A. 22201   Helpline 1-800-950-6264

Ontario Peer Development Initiative (formerly Consumer Survivor Development Initiative)
2160 Yonge Street
Toronto, Ontario M4S 2Z3   Phone (416) 484-8785
(This organization can provide information on consumer initiatives in your local area.)